Pastor Jorine

God Bless
you

Prophetess
Jennifer
Ava
Yes 2021

A
Fruitful Life
Is A
Spiritual Life

By
Sametta Brown

This book is dedication to

God

in the name of Jesus

and written by the leading of the Holy Ghost.

May God continually bless all whom have touched my life and helped the Fruit of the Spirit to grow within me and manifest itself through me.

But the fruit of the Spirit is

LOVE,
Joy,
Peace,
Longsuffering,
Gentleness,
Goodness,
Faith,
Meekness,
Temperance:

against such there is no law.

Galatians 5:22-23

Table of Contents

I am the true vine,
and my Father is the husbandman.

John 15:1

Preface

Isn't it amazing how something can go from small, medium, large and then all the X's? We become so amazed at the size on the outside that we forget that the development on the inside is what actually created what is seen.

Every aspect of our lives begins like a seed – small and waiting to yield.

But what does it take to grow in the Lord?
Where does this Spiritual Growth come from?
Am I supposed to use what I already have to grow spiritually?
What happens when I stop growing spiritually?
How does this growth benefit me?
How long does this growth process take?

As we seek the answers to these questions, we realize that the potential we have within us to grow has a direct effect on the lives of others as well as representing our Father.

Now some of you may be saying, "Uh the Fruit of the Spirit is milk." But if you can't operate in the first characteristics of the growth of the Spirit then your life is clabber and you need this bone strengthening word so you can take some things in the natural and be an example of how a child of God matures gracefully. Because remember God is a Spirit and those who are Spiritual are able to abstain, receive instruction, turn the cheek and stand in the midst of trials and tribulations. So what you *think* is milk could really be meat that you haven't been able to digest.

Every branch in me that beareth not fruit he taketh away: and every branch that beareth fruit, he purgeth it, that it may bring forth more fruit.

John 15:2

Definitions to help bring Revelation

(Definitions taken from Dictionary.com and 1828 Webster Dictionary)

SEED

The substance, animal or vegetable that nature prepares for the reproduction and conservation of the species. The seeds of plants are a deciduous part, containing the rudiments of a new vegetable. In some cases, the seeds constitute the fruit or valuable part of plants, as in the case of wheat and other esculent grain; sometimes the seeds are enclosed in fruit, as in apples and melons. When applied to animal matter, it has no plural.

That from which anything springs; first principle; original; as the seeds of virtue or vice.

Progeny; offspring; children; descendants; as the seed of Abraham; the seed of David. In this sense, the word is applied to one person, or to any number collectively, and admits of the plural form; but rarely used in the plural.

Race; generation; birth

VINE

The long slender stem of any plant that trails on the ground, or climbs and supports itself by winding round a fixed object, or by seizing any fixed thing with its tendrils or claspers.

Thus we speak of the hop vine, the bean vine, the vines of melons, squashes, pumpkins, and other encurbitaceous plants.

BRANCH

The shoot of a tree or other plant; a limb; a bough shooting from the stem, or from another branch or bough. Johnson restricts the word to a shoot from a main bough, but the definition warranted neither by etymology nor usage.

A division of a main stem, supporting the leaves and fructification.

A line of family descent stemming from a particular ancestor, as distinguished from some other line or lines from the same stock; a division of a family.

To divide into separate parts or subdivisions; diverge: The main road branches off to the left.

To expand or extend, as business activities: The bank has plans to branch throughout the state.

BRANCH WATER
Water in or from a branch, creek, stream, etc.; pure, natural water.

FRUIT

In a more limited sense, the produce of a tree or other plant; the last production for the propagation or multiplication of its kind; the seed of plants, or the part that contains the seeds; as wheat, rye, oats, apples, quinces, pears, cherries, acorns, melons, &c.

Production; that which is produced.

The fruit of the spirit is in all goodness, and righteousness, and truth.

Eph. 5.

The produce of animals; offspring; young; as the fruit of the womb, of the loins, of the body.

Effect or consequence.

They shall eat the fruit of their doings. Isa. 3.

Advantage; profit; good derived.

Any product of plant growth useful to humans or animals.

The edible part of a plant developed from a flower, with any accessory tissues, as the peach, mulberry or banana.

PRUNE

To lop or cut off the superfluous branches of trees, to make them bear better fruit or grow higher, or to give them a more handsome and regular appearance.

CUT

To separate the parts of any body by an edged instrument, either by striking, as with an ax, or by sawing or rubbing; to make a gash, incision or notch, which separates the external part of a body, as to cut the flesh.

It signifies also, to cut into pieces; to sever or divide; as, to cut timber in the forest. But when an entire separation of the body is intended, it is usually followed by off, down, asunder, in two, in pieces, or other word denoting such severance.

WEED

A valueless plant growing wild, especially one that grows on cultivated ground to the exclusion or injury of the desired crop.

Any undesirable or troublesome plant, especially one that grows profusely where it is not wanted: The vacant lot was covered with weeds.

To root out or remove a weed or weeds
To remove as being undesirable, inefficient, or superfluous to weed out
inexperienced players.

Now ye are clean through the word which I have spoken unto you.

Abide in me, and I in you.

John 15:3-4

Seeds that Produce Godly Results

When you think of it, we could consider ourselves as a package of seeds that have been planted in the earth so that this world can receive nourishment required to experience the manifested glory of our Lord. This requires that we complete the development process to be Godly fruit.

First, let's recognize from where the growth that produces righteous results come from – The True Vine.

James 15:1I am the true vine, and my Father is the husbandman.
  2Every branch in me that beareth not fruit he taketh away: and every branch that beareth fruit, he purgeth it, that it may bring forth more fruit.
  3Now ye are clean through the word which I have spoken unto you.
  4Abide in me, and I in you. As the branch cannot bear fruit of itself, except it abide in the vine; no more can ye, except ye abide in me.
  5I am the vine, ye are the branches: He that abideth in me, and I in him, the same bringeth forth much fruit: for without me ye can do nothing.

  6If a man abide not in me, he is cast forth as a branch, and is withered; and men gather them, and cast them into the fire, and they are burned.
  7If ye abide in me, and my words abide in you, ye shall ask what ye will, and it shall be done unto you.
  8Herein is my Father glorified, that ye bear much fruit; so shall ye be my disciples.

Jesus coming to earth is the natural side of a spiritual revelation. As The Vine He came and lived with us in the earth realm and among us so that we could learn from His example. But our growth through Jesus means that, as a seed, we become engrafted in Him, exposed, strengthened to endure and grow to cover and hold others who don't have the strength and guidance. So as Christians, we have Jesus working on the inside with the hand of the Lord upon us as the Spirit of God helps us grow and be fully functional mature individuals.

The seed (us) must be willing to break out of our shell (pride, hatred, envy, etc.) to get to the vine, as well as be ready to receive all that is necessary so that we can reach our full potential.

When we come out of the shell – our state of flesh – and get into the supernatural incubator, we allow the Holy Spirit to develop inside and begin to manifest the attributes of God, which is called Bearing Fruit. The only way to do that is to fully master the process of development and grow consistently in the Lord.

Seeds are small compared to the outcome of what it was created to produce. So why do we want to be considered mature without the complete nurturing, weathering and testing of our being? Well, one answer would be that we all have the capability of being great in whatever area, but we don't take the time to perfect each stage that it takes to understand the reason why we were placed on earth. And that's when we allow things on the outside (life, emotions, relationships and so on) to come and overtake what is on the inside causing us to have to be reseeded. Why the reseeding? Well we must get back in the right place, to do the right thing so we can grow and be complete in God.

As a seed stays in place, it takes root and branches out into unknown territory. That's where the "True Vine" is just waiting on us. When we grow into the True Vine, our spirit bears witness with God's Spirit (the Holy Spirit) and we are guided, instructed, corrected, led and fed. But the way we go is what determines what the outcome will be. That is why God sent Jesus for us to have a place to hide, grow, and learn to be internally intoxicated with righteous responses to the elements in life that try to overtake our production and maturing in the Fruit of the Holy Spirit.

One way of explaining the Fruit of the Spirit is to say that it is the fullness of God that compels us to say and do what Jesus did which is what God expects of us as His children. For example, naturally we sometimes feel like we can't go "another further' (as the saints of old would say)," but as we stay in the True Vine, trust God and declare The Word *"Let the weak say I am strong."* *(Joel 3:10),* we go past our natural ability and are strengthened to complete the task at hand.

Let's Grow......

In the natural I wouldn't allow you to cuss/curse me out without some type of retaliation, even when I know the word says, *"Vengeance is mine says the Lord."* *(Romans 12:19).* But being connected AND in The Vine I humble myself.

That promotes spiritual growth and I decide to choice praying pray for your deliverance because you know not what you do. And my obedience to God's Word pleases Him and keeps me from going to hell. Ok, here's another example that touches each and every one of us. In the natural realm one wouldn't speak to someone who has hurt a family member, but as we live a Spiritual life and remain fruitful we do not show a rotten attitude through our words or actions. We truly love, are kind and have genuine joy when we see that person. That us allowing the Holy Spirit to work in us to function in that manner because that is definitely NOT how our flesh would respond.

A *"Fruitful"* life in God produces deliverance, a liberty in our character that doesn't lock us up as the state hospital does in the natural realm to those sometimes labeled "Fruity." Being attached and not boxed in, releases us to flow in the liberty of which we have been called to ... forever. *(Galatians 5:1, Romans 8:21)*

Keeping one's self in The Vine guarantees that we receive the nutrients needed to grow. But we also reap a harvest by staying planted and not uprooting ourselves which in turn causes loss of time and things in life. This kind of uprooting requires us to humble ourselves and repent for complete restoration and repositioning.

Staying Covered

As You grow Inwardly

Just as natural seeds are covered with a shell, we, as children, have been protected from the outside elements/weeds by our parents, teachers, mentors, etc., and others until we come "of age," as the world calls it. Then we think we are grown enough to step out on our own not realizing that we still need to be covered but from a different position in life. That is why it is so important that when we do come into our own and leave the homes of our natural parents we must remember that we are not alone as a child of God. We are covered even the more by natural/spiritual parents and ultimately by the True Vine.

Remember growing in The True Vine means you are covered, nurtured and producing life that pleases God and manifests the promises based upon the obedience to God's Word. There are many vines that would love for us to take up residence in them and some of us have by taking advice from people who don't have wisdom, don't have an effective testimony or at least a good life. Come on, you KNOW who I am referring to – the relative who never has anything good to say but always has advice for you, the friend who is always in confusion but finds enough time to want to counsel you. Or the man/woman of God whose testimonies are always down trodden but they want to tell you how to come through. OK, I will stop ...

Thank God for His unfailing love, Jesus interceding for us and The Holy Spirit just waiting on us to grow in Him. For when the weeds of life come and we acknowledge that we are headed wrong because of our actions and conversation we have a place in Him to regroup, refocus and redirect ourselves from the weeded areas and wrong paths of life so that we grown into the place where we belong. By taking root and being covered in the right place, The True Vine, we are able to receive instruction, stay focused and confidently produce Spiritual Fruit.

God also gives us the right place of covering through Spiritual Parents as well as His Word. Through the Word of God we are able to engraft ourselves to the builder, restorer and repairer. Then we're able to know our position and the production that is to take place. Now remember, this does not happen without pruning, cutting and nurturing, which is for our own good. We use the Word of God to run a diagnosis test on ourselves to make sure we are in place, we are functioning and the fruit that we bear is good.
Doing what is right keeps us covered in the Grace of God and His mercy so that a worse thing won't come upon us. Being bearers of the Fruit of the Spirit makes us individually and collectively the righteousness of God with the blood of Jesus cleansing us, the Spirit of God flowing through us as His oil lubricates us.

Everything in life grows, but how we grow is the important aspect of development. Assessing the various stages in our lives and what/who we are attached to plays an integral part in our Christian walk. When people see us there shouldn't be anything stale, old or stagnant about us. But as natural circumstances take a toll on us we sometimes uncover our roots, pull away from the vine we are attached to and destroy the production that has taken place on the inside.

We, as individuals, have a responsibility in developing our spirit through God's Spirit so that we don't die. As you continue to read and study this book, you will realize there are more opportunities for the Holy Spirit to speak to you that will cut or trim out the bad and make room for plenty of fruitful and prosperous manifestations: naturally and spiritually.

Yes Child of God, we are all well able to be Spiritual all the time; remember our example is Jesus who learned, as He was on earth, to stay in the vein and continue maturing to not just for his gain, but for those who follow. *(Though he were a Son, yet learned he obedience by the things which he suffered; Hebrews 5:8)*

For us to do that we shouldn't just read the Word of God and be full of knowledge, but apply/obey the Word, everyday so that we produce/fruit and exemplify God. That means we will be ripe, ready, righteous – fit for the Master's use.

Oh yes! He wants to use each and every one of us just as he used Job, Daniel, David, Ruth and so on.
His use of us lets the world know that we are able to manifest His characteristics, branch out and change the world around us.

How?

When the weed of hate rolls in, love springs forth and takes over, *Love covers a multitude of sins. I Peter 4:8   Proverbs 10:12*

That's God and growth in Him. He's got you covered!

When the weed of unforgiveness creeps in, forgiveness will undo the wrapping that would try to stunt the development of maturity in the things of God.

That's God and growth in Him. He's got you covered!

When depression tries to overtake us we gird up our loins and remind ourselves that "the joy of the Lord is our strength (Nehemiah 8:10) and we speak life to ourselves.

That's God and growth in Him. He's got you covered!

Staying in The True Vine means that when turbulence shakes the core of our being, we are able to continue in the Way of the Lord. The peace of God comes in and fills us in the areas that weeds would try to tear us apart –But in God we are kept and covered!

Now let me say this, doing the "right" thing or, in this case, the "fruitful thing," is not always received but it is the righteous action that reveals growth to God and those watching our every move.

You know just as well as I do that those of the world aren't dumb or totally unlearned concerning the Word of God. They expect great things and mannerisms that are different from them. When one says they are "of God" His characteristics are expected to be manifested in the world by us, the Children of God, in a fruitful way ... growing and growing and growing.

As we show Christlike characteristics, instead of acting like the old man that some never seem to forget, we are letting all know that it is possible to change our responses to worldly matters. That is what shall be remembered and causes a conviction or metamorphosis in the lives of others which draws them to The True Vine, Jesus, and produces fruitful change in them -- what people see on the outside because of the shift that has taken place on the inside.

But we can't even become as strong as a branch until the deadness of life falls off and we have a new covering with our dependency on the Lord just as a baby with parents. Staying in the True Vine means you have access and the ability to know what, when, where and how to develop so the Fruit is not just smelled or displayed but tasted and well worth it.

John 15:3 Now ye are clean through the word which I have spoken unto you. 4 Abide in me, and I in you.

Getting Rid of the Weeds
to Succeed

Why must I be in the right position? Why can't I just be put back in and grow? Well, you were created for a purpose and filled with potential to manifest God's plan. We can't effectively make a difference in the lives of others if we are all over the place in our actions, emotions and responses to others. So when we are spiritually out of position we can't handle or fulfill the ordained assignments for our life. Going from a seed to a branch not only means the outside changes but also the inside must change to reveal the strength, longevity and bountifulness of a branch.

There are many things, which we will call weeds, but they all have one agenda – to uproot, move us and break stage of development in the True Vine so we won't mature.

When you are shaky, fragile and/or wimpy the weathering conditions of life will come to overtake, wound, hurt, drain and destroy you as well as all that are attached to you. Remember that is Satan's job, to kill, steal and destroy so that you don't reach the next season/level in your life. It is so important to stay in The True Vine, get The Word in, and out of us to be strengthened and able to stand our ground under the various stages of storms. We want to be a branch able to produce righteous fruit that is not poked through by the worms of life or uncovered by the elements of our atmosphere.

Our position in Jesus makes us sensitive to the alarms that go off when we are in potential danger-weeds coming up. In Him we are sheltered to yield a harvest but we must continue in the way of the Lord as not to destroy our progress or have it destroyed by outside elements.

Now remember the definition of weeds. They grow wild, waste space as well as take up your time for having to deal with them. We don't want to be entangled in them and stunt our growth due to the fact that WE wasted time. We don't want to be rotten or no good to those we were assigned to help grow spiritually. The development of Spiritual Fruit in us has us look good, speak sound counsel and demonstrate the Love of God to the world.

But don't think we are just to look good, smell good and taste good for our own benefit. No ma'am. No sir. We must take note of our own actions and not entangle ourselves with weeds so that others can see that the growth process even among weeds is possible. (*And be not conformed to this world: but be ye transformed by the renewing of your mind, that ye may prove what is that good, and acceptable, and perfect, will of God. Romans 12:2*)

Even though it hurts our flesh, pulling away from the weeds works for our good and we have nothing to be ashamed of just because we act and look different.

Hurt to the flesh? Oh yes, we all know how man's ways can cut us to the core but God's action of cutting the fat (the part of us that is no good and weighs us down) helps lift us as we bleed out all the impurities that would infect our soul and spirit. And as the Lord prunes us, we must also prune and cut off things for ourselves, meaning our characteristics, places we go, people we speak to and even to the point of cutting off.

There is a difference and I will put it like this: To cut off is to be done with and not to see that type of growth again. While to be pruned means trimmed back to where there is hope and the opportunity for growth to take place from the area that is still good. Think about when you go to the beautician or barber shop. When the person servicing you trims (prunes) the bad areas of your hair, you are pleased because what was necessary was done. But when someone "gets happy" with your hair and just starts cutting with no restraint, then the good and the bad gets cut and let's just say there is no tip (reward) for the service.

That's why Spiritual growth in the Holy Ghost is very important. We must know what process we are in and how to handle it. Everyday life can have us entangled and be overwhelming if we don't know how to take the good and leave the bad. Individually we must weed out and fertilize ourselves with the Word of God to push forth and produce fruit with anchored roots.

In those times we don't go through life fooling ourselves and thinking all is well when life's elements have contaminated our production of being Spiritually Fruitful. That's why staying in and growing on the True Vine helps bring a divine result. Maturing from the seed to grow into the True Vine helps stabilize us, protect us and direct us. We learn and live a life of love, joy, peace, longsuffering and so on without going back into hatred, strife, envying and so forth. *(Gal. 5)*

Think of a car which is created to run only on the road, but it is driven every once in while a on rough terrain as if it is a Jeep/truck. After a while parts of the car will be out of position and/or off balance because it has not been treated right due to wild driving, not being where it was ordained to be and then no check-ups to maintain it. The vehicle becomes unable to function to its full potential or last the expected life span. The same is true of us if we are out of position and go in a path, that is not prepared for our lives.

We must be dedicated to daily confront and address areas of emotions and actions that try to set up residence in the soil of our soul to affect our spirit. Yep, there are some people who grow in adultery, wrath, witchcraft, idolatry and all the things that are weeds to our spirit according to the Word of God. *(Gal 5:16-21)*. BUT we have been given all the tools we need to deal with everything that arises in our lives everyday.

What tools you may ask? Use the tool of "Faith: Believe." Fight the *good* fight *of faith* for your life to cut/prune off everything and/or person that tries to take up territory or push you out of what God has given you. Use your faith as a *hammer* to beat out, a *saw* to cut off, a *nail* to stick with what God says or a *drill* to drive out the enemy in Jesus' Name! Other tools to use include *Praise* that will scatter/gather, *Peace* which will shut out all disturbances and the powerful tool of *Love*.

Increasing our *faith in God* is detrimental to our spiritual life and keeps us grounded in the Lord so that we not only live a blessed life but are able to restore and strengthen our brother/sister in love because we have matured in the *Fruit of the Spirit.*

As the branch cannot bear fruit of itself, except it abide in the vine; no more can ye, except ye abide in me.

John 15:3-4

The Fruit Of the Spirit

Precious Child of God

  As a farmer diligently tends to his fields and reaps bountifully from his labor, we, as Christians, must continue to plant the Word of God in our lives every day to grow spiritually. When we deposit this essential seed, The Word of God, we successfully reap a fruitful life: spiritually and naturally. And how do we do this?

*1. **Write down the scripture that contains the fruit that is specifically emphasized.***

*2. **Study God's Word by reading the chapter of the scripture that is emphasized so you can get the full meaning and reference other scriptures.***

*3. **Live God's Word**.*

*4. **Manifest God's Word***

Let's Grow...

And the Lord said to Moses, Write thou these words...
Exodus 34:27

    1. **Write down the scripture that contains the fruit that is specifically emphasized.** All through the Bible God instructs us, His children, to write down His Words because they are His promises, and intimate communication with us. *(De. 6:9, Pr 3:3, 7:3, Je 30:2)*
.

Study to shew thyself approved ... 2 Timothy 2:15

    2. **Study God's Word by reading the chapter of the scripture that is emphasized so you can get the full meaning and reference other scriptures.** God's Word was given to us to know how to live. That means we must make and take time to learn what God's Word says concerning every area of our lives. *(I Thessalonians 4:10-12)*

Let's Mature...

Abide in me and I in you.
St. John 15:4-7

3. **Live God's Word**. The more we study God's Word, the more His Spirit will be manifested in everything we do. Because Jesus is our example and He lived on earth we know that the Fruit of the Spirit in us makes the Word of God completely applicable. *(I Peter 2:24, 4:6)*

For the earnest expectation of the creature waiteth
for the manifestation of the sons of God. Romans 8:19

4. **Manifest God's Word.** Produce what you have studied and show the world that the Great I AM flows through you in every situation. *(Romans 8:23)*

Study this manifested fruit and learn what the Word of God says is required of you, what is within you and what is promised to you.

LOVE - that's *everlasting*...

When God inspired man to write about the Fruit of the Spirit isn't is amazing that He started with Love.

The very characteristics that caused Him to save us. The very feeling that makes man's heart change. The very essence of His being and our existence – LOVE.

Ephesians 4:11-16

Deuteronomy 7:9-15

I John 4:7-21

John 15:9-13

Galatians 2:20-21

Jude 20-25

Jeremiah 31:1-4

My Inspiration from the Holy Ghost

Joy - that comes *from JESUS*

You will feel this when pure love exists within. Others will know this by the actions you display. God strengthens and builds you with this emotion through every phase of life.

Nehemiah 8:10-16

John 15:11

Luke 8:13

Proverbs 15:23

Galatians 5:22-26

II Thessalonians 1:11-12

Psalm 107:1-32

My Inspiration from the Holy Ghost

Peace- that *mends* the b ʳo k ᵉ n   p i e c ᵉ s

Not a feeling per se but a knowing that even when things don't come together as you plan, the Spirit quiets you and the Lord's orchestrated will is in control.

Job 22:21-23

Hebrews 13:20-21

Philippians 4:4-7

Leviticus 26:6-8

Isaiah 40:10-11

Galatians 5:14-26

I Thessalonians 2:1-9

My Inspiration from the Holy Ghost

Longsuffering - that's patiently *enduring*

Never giving up on a cause, purpose or who is so dear. As time ticks away the end of a thing is worth the wait and far more priceless.

Colossians 3:8-17

Ephesians 4:1-6

II Timothy 4:1-5

Galatians 5:14-26

II Peter 3:1-9

Colossians 1:1-17

II Corinthians 6:1-10

My Inspiration from the Holy Ghost

Gentleness - that's *graceful*

The power to discern and delicately handle the heart of man even when you do not understand his actions.

II Samuel 22:31-36

Psalm 18:30-35

II Timothy 2:18-26

James 3:13-18

Galatians 6:15-16

Ephesians 2:14-18

Isaiah 26:3

My Inspiration from the Holy Ghost

Goodness - that's *God's nature*

Expressing the wholesome characteristics of God toward mankind by making excellent choices in life that radiate God's nature.

Psalm 23:1-6

Jeremiah 33:1-9

Ephesians 5:1-12

Romans 11:16-23

Isaiah 12:1-6

Romans 15:8-13

Jeremiah 31:10-14

My Inspiration from the Holy Ghost

Faith - that's *assurance*

A Believer who doesn't give up but expects nothing less than the promise: God's guaranteed outcome.

Hebrews 11:1-40

Habakkuk 2:1-4

James 1:1-8

Romans 14:1-4

Galatians 5:22-26

John 11:33-44

Col. 1:19-23

My Inspiration from the Holy Ghost

Meekness - that's *not weakness*

At a time when you want to be defensive, you choose to refrain from responding according to the dictation of your flesh.

Galatians 6:1-2

Ephesians 4:1-3

I Timothy 6:1-11

I Peter 3:12-16

Colossians 3:8-17

Titus 3:1-7

II Timothy 2:24-26

My Inspiration from the Holy Ghost

Temperance - that's *restraining*

Putting in place actions and emotions that would take you in the direction of untimely, destructive results that impact the lives of all around you.

Acts 24:24-27

II Peter 1:3-9

Galatians 5:16-26

Proverbs 16:32

Romans 6:12-18

Proverbs 23:29-35

Ephesians 5:17-21

My Inspiration from the Holy Ghost

But there is a spirit in man:
and the inspiration of the Almighty giveth
them understanding.

Job 32:8

My Time of Re-dedication for Regeneration

As you prepare to cultivate your life in the Word of God don't allow yourself or others to root up your work or discourage you from being grounded in the Lord.

For God *so loved* the world, that *he gave* his only begotten Son,

that whosoever believeth in him should not perish,

but have everlasting life.   *John 3:16*

But what saith it? The *word* is nigh thee, even in thy mouth, and in thy

heart: that is the *word of faith,* which we preach;

That if thou shall <u>*confess* with thy mouth</u> the Lord Jesus,

and shalt <u>*believe* in thine heart</u> that God hath raised him from the dead,

thou shalt be saved.

<u>*For with the heart*</u> man believeth unto righteousness;

and <u>*with the mouth*</u> confession is made unto salvation.

For the scripture saith,

<u>*Whosoever believeth*</u> in him shall not be ashamed.

Romans 10:8-11

Prayer: *Thank you God for loving me and giving your son Jesus to be our example, covering and intercessor. I welcome your Holy Spirit to dwell in me even the more so that I am a fruitful vessel to be used by thee.*

As you begin to flourish in the Lord, make sure you are:

- Going to a church where the Word of God is being taught, preached and lived

- Studying the Word of God for yourself on a daily basis

- Giving God what you haven't been giving Him so that you can grow and manifest beauty, life, abundance and love

- Faithful as unto God at home, work, and church

- Trusting God's word in you to keep and carry you through life

About the Author

Sametta Brown, also known as "The King's Kid," is the daughter of Samuel Brown and Maggie Lee Brown. This woman of God wears many hats, which include being a radio announcer, producer (*Mission Gospel Train*) and television host for the Christian Family Network Television Station (*Good Neighbors*).

She attributes her foundational nurturing, corrected and strengthening in the Word of God to her mother and grandmother, Rozena Lee.

Sametta Brown is the spiritual daughter of Apostles James and Nyjah Newton Prophetic Judah Kingdom Intl, Lawton, Oklahoma.